Built for Speed

The World's Fastest Trucks

by Glen and Karen Bledsoe

Consultant:
Robert Vizcarra
Media Relations Manager
National Hot Rod Association

CAPSTONE
HIGH-INTEREST
BOOKS

an imprint of Capstone Press
Mankato, Minnesota

Capstone High-Interest Books are published by Capstone Press
151 Good Counsel Drive, P.O. Box 669, Mankato, Minnesota 56002
http://www.capstone-press.com

Library of Congress Cataloging-in-Publication Data
Bledsoe, Glen.
    The world's fastest trucks/by Glen and Karen Bledsoe.
    p. cm.—(Built for speed)
    Includes bibliographical references and index.
    Summary: Discusses the history and development of some of the world's fastest
trucks, describing the specific features and specifications of such vehicles as racing
pickups, semi-trucks, monster trucks, and jet-powered trucks.
    ISBN 0-7368-1062-5
    1. Trucks—Juvenile literature. 2. Truck racing—Juvenile literature.
3. Automobiles, Racing—Juvenile literature. [1. Trucks. 2. Truck racing.]
I. Bledsoe, Karen E. II. Title. III. Built for speed (Mankato, Minn.)
TL230.15 .B58 2002
629.224—dc21   2001003439

Editorial Credits
Leah K. Pockrandt, editor; Karen Risch, product planning editor; Timothy Halldin,
    cover designer, interior layout designer, and interior illustrator; Katy Kudela,
    photo researcher

Photo Credits
Action Images/Dave & Bev Huntoon, 24, 27, 28
Alice & Bob Howard, 33, 39 (top), 40
C.C. Racing, Ltd., 16, 38 (top)
Contract Freighters, Inc., 20, 38 (bottom)
Gale Banks Engineering, 15
Kenworth of Australia, 43
Louise Ann Noeth, 23
Nalani T. Seydel, 35, 39 (bottom)
NHRA/National Dragster, 8, 11
Photri-Microstock/Mark E. Gibson, 4; Photri-Microstock, 18
Unicorn Stock Photos/Russell R. Grundke, cover, 30
www.ronkimball/stock.com, 7, 12

1 2 3 4 5 6 07 06 05 04 03 02

Table of Contents

Chapter 1

Fast Trucks

Transportation methods used by people have changed during the past century. In the past, people used wagons pulled by horses and oxen to carry cargo from one place to another. Today, people use trucks to transport cargo. They use semitrucks to haul large supplies of products across long distances. They use pickup trucks to carry small loads.

Most trucks are not built to travel at high speeds. But some people race trucks. Racers make changes to trucks to make the trucks travel much faster. Racers may build trucks with powerful racing engines. Some build trucks with jet-powered engines.

People use semitrucks to haul large supplies.

Types of Truck Races

Many kinds of truck races exist. Some drivers compete against other drivers on racetracks. Other drivers try to set speed records on large, flat areas such as dry lake beds.

Some drivers race trucks on straight tracks. Straight track races often measure how fast a truck is traveling at a certain distance from the starting line. A common distance used is one-fourth mile (400 meters). Racers call this distance a "quarter mile." A race also may measure a truck's average or ending speed.

Many racetracks are shaped like a circle or oval. Trucks must turn smoothly to perform well on oval or circular tracks.

Some truck races take place on rugged terrain. Drivers may have to drive their trucks up hills and over rocks. Trucks that race on these courses must have strong frames. They also must have special shock absorbers. These devices lessen the bumps of driving over rough surfaces.

Different classes of truck races exist. Each class has its own rules. Some classes allow changes to the cab's shape. A driver sits in the truck's cab. Other classes may not allow changes.

Some drivers race on straight or oval tracks.

Timing Associations

Drivers must compete at land speed races called trials to make or break speed records. Organizations that record speed trials have rules that drivers must follow to qualify their times. These organizations include the Southern California Timing Association (SCTA), the Utah Salt Flats Racing Association (USFRA), and the East Coast Timing Association (ECTA).

Racing trucks have aerodynamic designs.

The timing organizations plan land speed racing events. The USFRA helps organize the World of Speed Week at the Bonneville Salt Flats. This dry lake bed is near Salt Lake City, Utah.

Designed for Speed
Different elements help trucks travel fast. These elements include engines, fuels, and

aerodynamic designs. Aerodynamic designs reduce wind resistance. This force slows down moving objects.

Fast trucks need powerful engines. An engine's power is measured in horsepower. Trucks with powerful engines often can travel at higher speeds than trucks with less powerful engines.

Fuel can increase an engine's power. Most factory truck engines burn either straight gasoline or diesel fuel. But some racers modify their engines. They change their engines to allow them to burn other fuels. Some racers use pure methyl alcohol in their trucks. This fuel also is called methanol. Some racers add nitrous oxide gas into their engine with their fuel. Methanol and nitrous oxide help to increase an engine's power.

Trucks are shaped to carry cargo. Most truck trailers are shaped like a rectangle. But trucks with trailers cannot travel fast. Fast trucks need aerodynamic designs to allow air to flow smoothly over and around them.

Smooth edges and sloped, flat areas help reduce wind resistance and allow trucks to travel faster.

The ability of a truck to turn is called "handling." Several features affect handling. These features include the engine's horsepower and width of the wheelbase. The wheelbase is the distance between the front and rear wheel axles. The weight of the vehicle also can affect the truck's handling.

Racing Safety

Safety is important when driving at high speeds. A crash could seriously injure or kill a racer. Drivers and trucks have special safety equipment.

Drivers wear safety equipment and clothing. All racers wear helmets to protect their heads. Safety clothing is made from a fire-resistant material called Nomex.

Racing trucks must have good handling.

Many racing organizations require drivers to wear a safety harness. This strap holds the driver in place like a seatbelt does.

Some racing trucks have roll cages. These steel bars are located behind the racer's seat. Roll bars protect the driver if the truck rolls over.

Chapter 2

Racing
Pickup Trucks

Many drivers race pickup trucks. Some drivers race standard pickup trucks. Others race trucks that are specially designed and built.

Factory-built Racing Pickups

The SVT F-150 Lightning is a performance pickup truck. Ford Motor Company manufactures the truck. The Lightning has a top speed of 140 miles (225 kilometers) per hour. It can reach a speed of 60 miles (97 kilometers) per hour in less than 7 seconds. This speed is called "zero to 60." Only some truck dealers in the United States and Canada sell the SVT F-150 Lightning.

The Lightning has a top speed of 140 miles (225 kilometers) per hour.

Many people claim that the GMC Syclone is the fastest standard pickup truck. The Syclone will run a quarter-mile in 13.4 to 14.3 seconds. GMC also makes a similar model called the Typhoon. The Typhoon will run the quarter-mile in 13.8 to 14.7 seconds. The Syclone and Typhoon will reach 60 miles (97 kilometers) per hour in 5 to 5.5 seconds.

GMC made a limited number of Syclones and Typhoons. It made about 3,000 Syclones and about 4,700 Typhoons in the early 1990s.

Cars usually are more lightweight and faster than trucks. But the Syclone is faster than many high-performance sports cars. Car magazines and GMC dealerships have sponsored races with Syclones against Ferraris. The Syclones won zero to 60 and quarter-mile tests.

Gale Banks and the Syclone

Gale Banks began working on cars when he was a boy. At 16, he built his first engine.

Today, Banks owns a company called Gale Banks Engineering. In 1990, the company modified a GMC Syclone pickup. Banks' truck traveled 210 miles (338 kilometers) per hour at the Bonneville Salt Flats. It set a world speed

Gale Banks' Syclone was the first truck to exceed 200 miles (322 kilometers) per hour.

record for a pickup truck. It also became the first pickup truck to travel faster than 200 miles (322 kilometers) per hour.

Glen May and the Cranberry Connection

Glen May owns one of the fastest Pro Modified drag-racing pickups. These trucks started as street trucks. But mechanics have changed the engines and designs of them. Drag-racing vehicles race on straight courses. These courses are one-fourth mile (400 meters) long. May's truck is a modified

Glen May's Cranberry Connection set a record speed for a pickup truck.

Ford Ranger called the Cranberry Connection. The Cranberry Connection has a sloping design with curved edges. The truck's body also is very close to the ground.

The Cranberry Connection has a super charged Ford Hemi engine for extra power and speed. A super charger is an air pump that is attached to the engine by a belt. The air pump allows more air to enter the engine and increase the engine's power.

In 1999, the truck reached a record speed of 214 miles (344 kilometers) per hour in 6.395 seconds. That same year, the International Hot Rod Association (IHRA) gave the Cranberry Connection the Best Engineered Pro Car award.

Racing Pickup Trucks
In the past, Pro Modified or Pro Stock trucks were not common in drag racing. Few drag racing truck rules existed when truck drag racing first began. But drag-racing pickups now are gaining acceptance. Racing associations have developed more rules to maintain safety during races.

Like other race vehicles, Pro Modified and Pro Stock trucks have special vehicle designs. These trucks have a racing chassis. A chassis is the frame on which a truck's body is built. Pro Modified and Pro Stock trucks have aerodynamic bodies. The body also may have an unusual and creative design.

Pro Modified and Pro Stock trucks are expensive to build and maintain. These trucks can cost more than $120,000 to build. The engine alone can cost $50,000.

Chapter 3

Racing Semitrucks

Semitrucks are designed to carry heavy loads across long distances. A standard semitruck consists of a tractor that pulls a trailer. Semitrucks also are called tractor trailers and semis.

Semi tractors can pull different types of trailers. The most common trailers are enclosed and shaped like a rectangle. Others are long tanks that hold liquids. Some trailers are flat, open beds. Semitruck tractors can pull up to three trailers at one time.

Semis are powerful vehicles. They usually are not designed to travel faster than highway speeds. But some people have modified semitrucks to compete in races.

Semi tractors pull different types of trailers.

Red Racer "Flat Out" set a Class 8 speed record
in 1999.

Class 8 Trucks

A Class 8 truck is a heavy-duty semitruck.
It is powerful enough to haul heavy loads.
Some people modify Class 8 trucks to increase
their speed.

A Class 8 truck also is called a "Highway
Hauler." Trucks that race in the Highway Hauler
class are the closest of all racing trucks to
standard trucks. Highway Haulers must have
diesel-burning engines and be able to haul freight.

Red Racer "Flat Out"

In October 1999, Glenn Brown of Contract Freighters, Inc. set a Class 8 speed record. Brown drove a T2000 Kenworth named Red Racer "Flat Out." He reached 168 miles (270 kilometers) per hour. The Red Racer uses a 2,200-horsepower engine. Standard semi trucks have a 600-horsepower engine.

The Red Racer needs special equipment. The 20,000-pound (9,072-kilogram) Red Racer uses aircraft tires. Like most drag-racing vehicles, the truck uses parachutes to stop. These lightweight pieces of strong fabric are folded into a small pack at the truck's rear. The driver yanks a release cord at the end of the race to open the parachute. The parachute then quickly slows down the truck.

Joint Venture Freightliner

In 1998, a Freightliner semitruck called Joint Venture set the land speed record for modified diesel trucks. It traveled 224.163 miles (360.746 kilometers) per hour at the Bonneville Salt Flats. Longview Diesel and Interstate Wood Products co-own the truck.

The 1997 white Freightliner has a 4,000-horsepower diesel engine. The engine has four turbo-chargers. The Joint Venture has a backup parachute in case its brakes fail.

The truck needs special tires to help it reach high speeds. Joint Venture's front tires are from an F-15 jet fighter airplane. Its rear tires are from a Boeing 737 jet. The driver sits in a specially-designed roll cage.

The Phoenix

In 1996, The Phoenix set the world speed record for diesel trucks at 212.478 miles (341.941 kilometers) per hour. The truck became the SCTA World Record Unlimited Diesel truck.

Carl Heap owns The Phoenix. The 1943 International K-7 is in the Unlimited Diesel Class. It has a 4,000-horsepower engine. The truck uses Boeing 707 tires in the front and Boeing 727 tires in the back. In 1997, Heap failed to break his record when the truck caught fire at 237 miles (381 kilometers) per hour.

The Phoenix set a world record for diesel trucks.

In August 1998, Heap tried again to break the record. The Phoenix had reached a speed of 239 miles (385 kilometers) per hour at the end of the mile. But its engine was damaged. The Phoenix could not complete the second run needed to set the official record.

In August 2000, The Phoenix broke its own record. The truck reached a speed of 231.356 miles (372.321 kilometers) per hour.

Chapter 4

Racing Monster Trucks

Monster trucks are specially built pickup trucks. They have very large tires that make the body sit high off the ground. The driver's seat and steering wheel are in the middle of the truck's cab. The driver has to enter the cab through a hatch on the vehicle's underside. Monster trucks have a full roll cage in case they tip over. Some trucks also have a remote ignition interrupter switch. This switch allows a person to shut off the engine in case of an emergency.

Monster trucks are exhibition trucks. People use these trucks for special shows and races. People cannot drive them on the street because the trucks are too wide. People sometimes use

Monster trucks are specially built exhibition trucks.

monster trucks to jump over obstacles such as cars. Drivers also may crush cars or perform other stunts.

Some drivers also race monster trucks. Monster trucks can reach high speeds across short distances. These trucks quickly can reach a speed of 100 miles (161 kilometers) per hour.

Bigfoot: The First Monster Truck

Bob Chandler built the first monster truck. It was a four-wheel drive Ford F-250 pickup truck with oversized tires. Chandler called the truck "Bigfoot." In 1979, he displayed his truck at a car show in Denver, Colorado.

In 1981, Chandler decided to try rolling Bigfoot over some cars at a show. The audience enjoyed the performance. Other people soon built monster trucks to perform the same stunts. But soon, audiences grew tired of watching car-crushing events. Monster truck drivers started racing each other and tried new stunts.

Chandler now has more than 12 monster trucks. Each truck has a Bigfoot name. Bigfoot trucks cost more than $140,000 to build. The 1,200-horsepower engine can cost

Bigfoot was the first monster truck built and used for exhibition.

$35,000 or more. The trucks are painted with a special color-changing paint. This paint looks as if it changes color when viewed in certain light or at certain angles. Chandler and his crew may take from three months to one year to build a Bigfoot truck.

Bigfoot trucks are not the fastest monster trucks on a straight course. They can travel as fast as 80 miles (129 kilometers) per hour. But

Bear Foot is the fastest monster truck on a 300-yard (274-meter) track.

Bigfoot truck drivers can win races against other trucks. Bigfoot is the leading land speed record holder. Bigfoot trucks' engines also give them quicker starts on straight courses. Bigfoot trucks use methanol for fuel. The trucks burn between 2 and 3 gallons (7.6 and 11.4 liters) during each run.

Drivers also use Bigfoot trucks to jump over obstacles such as cars and airplanes. Bigfoot 14 set a world's record for the longest outdoor jump. In 1999, the truck jumped a distance of 141 feet, 10 inches (43.2 meters).

Fred Shafer and Bear Foot

Fred Shafer built a monster truck to challenge Bigfoot's popularity. The truck's name is "Bear Foot." Bear Foot is a modified Dodge Ram pickup with a 1,500-horsepower engine. It was one of the first monster trucks to use 66-inch (168-centimeter) tires. This size is now the standard for monster trucks.

Fred Shafer named the truck for his two pet American black bears. He often carried the bears in the back of the truck. People started calling the truck "Bear Foot."

Bear Foot has won the United States Hot Rod Association Monster Truck Racing Championship three times. Bear Foot is the fastest monster truck on a 300-yard (274-meter) track. It also holds the world record for an indoor jump. This jump was 119 feet, 2 inches (36.3 meters).

In 1997, Paul Shafer purchased Bear Foot from Fred Shafer. Paul now owns five Bear Foot trucks.

Chapter 5

Jet-Powered Trucks

Most trucks have engines that burn gasoline or methanol for fuel. But a few trucks have jet engines. These exhibition trucks are much faster than standard trucks.

Super Shockwave

The jet-powered Super Shockwave is so fast that it races against airplanes at shows. The airplanes fly above the truck as it drives down a runway. Super Shockwave holds the world record for trucks at 376 miles (605 kilometers) per hour. The truck's speed helped Super Shockwave earn the name "The World's Fastest Chevrolet."

Like other fast trucks, Super Shockwave is a custom-built vehicle. The truck has a 1957 Chevy fiberglass body. This strong, lightweight

People call Super Shockwave "The World's Fastest Chevrolet."

material is made from woven glass threads. The truck's body sits on a chromoly steel alloy chassis. This heavy, strong material is a mixture of two metals called chromium and molybdenum.

The truck's three Pratt & Whitney J34-48 jet engines produce 36,000 horsepower. The Super Shockwave uses 120 gallons (454 liters) of diesel fuel during each run. It weighs 6,800 pounds (3,084 kilograms) and is worth $500,000. The Super Shockwave uses two 14-foot (4.3-meter) parachutes to stop. It also carries two 16-foot (4.9-meter) parachutes for emergencies.

Les Shockley owns Super Shockwave. Ken High has been the truck's driver since 1992. High has made more than 900 runs in Super Shockwave.

Earthquake II
Earthquake II is a jet-powered semitruck. Bob and Alice Howard bought the truck from Phil Rini. Rini designed and built the original Earthquake I and II. Earthquake I was destroyed in an accident.

Earthquake II's jet engines push the truck faster than 300 miles (483 kilometers) per hour.

Only the roll cage survived. Rini used the roll cage in Earthquake II.

Earthquake II began as a 1995 Kenworth T600. It has wheels made from aluminum. Its engine is a GE J-79-2 jet engine. Earthquake II's engine produces 34,000 horsepower. The J-79-2 engine pushes Earthquake II faster than 300 miles (483 kilometers) per hour. A racing organization has not officially recorded the Earthquake II's speed. The owners perform at air shows for fun rather than for setting speed records.

At full speed, the engine burns about 10 gallons (38 liters) of fuel per second. During this time, the engine uses enough air to fill a 10,000-square-foot (929-square-meter) building. Earthquake II does not have a trailer. The fiery blast produced by the engine would burn anything behind the tractor.

A jet-powered semitruck cannot stop with ordinary brakes. The Earthquake II uses two 18-foot (5.5-meter) parachutes to stop.

Hawaiian Fire Department Fire Truck

The Hawaiian Fire Department jet-powered truck is called "The Fastest Truck in the World." It holds the world's speed record at 404.97 miles (651.72 kilometers) per hour. It also is ranked as the fifth fastest vehicle in the world.

The truck is custom-built. The truck's body looks like that of a 1940 Ford fire truck. But

The Hawaiian Fire Department jet-powered truck is the fastest truck in the world.

the truck is made of fiberglass and aluminum pieces. The truck cab is made of fiberglass. The truck's body is made of lightweight aluminum panels. The truck sits on a chromoly chassis. Most of the ladders, hoses, and other fire truck objects are from old fire trucks.

The truck is powered by two Rolls-Royce 601 Viper engines. The engines produce a total of 12,000 horsepower. The truck uses about 207 gallons (784 liters) of jet fuel for each run.

Shannen Thomas Seydel designed and built the truck. Seydel spent three years building the truck. He finished it in 1997. The Hawaiian Fire Department is not a real fire department. Seydel once was a fireman and also lived in Hawaii.

Seydel also is the truck's driver. Seydel made the first public run with the truck in 1997 in San Antonio, Texas. He set the speed record in 1998.

Seydel displays the truck at benefit shows across the United States. Money raised by the shows supports fire departments and helps children.

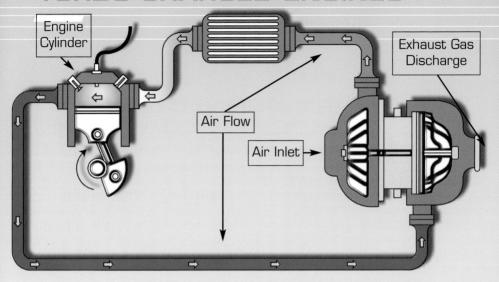

Engines get their power from burning a mixture of air and fuel. An engine's horsepower depends on its fuel and the amount of air pumped through the engine. Opening and closing the throttle usually controls this power. This device regulates the amount of fuel the engine receives.

A turbo-charged engine controls the amount of air pumped through the engine. The heat of an engine's exhaust normally is wasted. A turbo-charged engine uses the energy from the exhaust's heat to produce more power.

FAST FACTS

CRANBERRY CONNECTION

Owner:	Glen May
Make:	Modified Ford Ranger
Engine:	Super charged 526-cubic-inch Ford Hemi
Horsepower:	2,400
Top Speed:	214 miles (344 kilometers) per hour

RED RACER "FLAT OUT"

Owner:	Glenn Brown
Make:	T2000 model Kenworth
Engine:	Cummins K-series with dual turbochargers
Horsepower:	2,200
Top Speed:	168 miles (270 kilometers) per hour

EARTHQUAKE II

Owner: Bob and Alice Howard
Make: 1995 Kenworth T600
Engine: GE J-79-2 jet engine
Horsepower: 34,000
Top Speed: Faster than 300 miles (483 kilometers) per hour

HAWAIIAN FIRE DEPARTMENT JET-POWERED FIRE TRUCK

Owner: Shannen Thomas Seydel
Make: Custom-built fire truck based on a 1940 Ford fire truck body
Engines: Two Rolls-Royce 601 Viper engines
Horsepower: 12,000
Top Speed: 404.97 miles (651.72 kilometers) per hour

Chapter 6

The Future of Fast Trucks

Trucks' speeds have increased greatly over the years. Advances in technology allow designers to build trucks that travel faster than 400 miles (644 kilometers) per hour.

Improved Performance

New fuels may help trucks go even faster than today's trucks. Many trucks have turbo-charged engines. But some trucks now have engines that use nitrous oxide. These engines are very powerful. But they also are very dangerous. Drivers must pay attention to safety when operating these engines.

In 2000, a competition called FutureTruck 2000 demonstrated new truck features. These features

Designers will continue to create faster trucks.

may improve the performance of standard and racing trucks. Each team started with a Chevrolet Suburban sport-utility vehicle and $10,000.

The teams' goal was to change the vehicle to better use fuel and release less pollution. One team used a hydrogen fuel cell for power instead of a conventional gasoline engine. Hydrogen is a gas that can burn.

High-tech Trucks

The Kenworth Company recently released a standard semi called "The Truck of the Future." This truck is safer than many of today's trucks. It has a special electronics system in the steering wheel and control panel. This system reduces the amount of wiring in the truck by 75 percent. The truck's dashboard display looks like that of a large jet airplane. The display is on four computer screens instead of standard dials and gauges.

The driver can control many of the truck's functions with the screens. The truck uses an onboard Global Positioning System (GPS) to help the driver navigate. A collision warning system alerts the driver when other vehicles are too

The Truck of the Future uses less fuel than other semis.

close. Cameras mounted on the sides of the truck allow the driver to see all around the vehicle.

The truck's C-15 engine is electronically controlled. It produces 490 horsepower while using less fuel than other semis.

The new Kenworth semi shows how technology can improve trucks to increase performance and make them easier to operate. The technology used to create "The Truck of the Future" will help improve all trucks of the future.

Words to Know

accelerate (ak-SEL-uh-rate)—to gain speed

chassis (CHASS-ee)—the frame on which the body of a vehicle is built

chromoly (KROH-muh-lee)—a mixture of two metals called chromium and molybdenum; this material also is called "CrMo."

fiberglass (FYE-bur-glass)—a strong, lightweight material made from woven glass threads

horsepower (HORSS-pou-ur)—a unit that measures an engine's power

methanol (MEH-thuh-nawl)—a fuel made from alcohol

nitrous oxide (NEYE-truhss OK-side)—a gas made up of nitrogen and oxygen

throttle (THROT-uhl)—a valve in a vehicle's engine that opens to let steam, fuel, or fuel and air flow into the engine; the throttle controls the vehicle's speed.

To Learn More

The Encyclopedia of Awesome Machines.
   Brookfield, Conn.: Copper Beech
   Books, 1999.

Hintz, Martin and Kate Hintz. *Monster Truck*
   Drag Racing. Drag Racing. Mankato,
   Minn.: Capstone Books, 1996.

McAuliffe, Bill. *Off-Road Truck Racing.*
   MotorSports. Mankato, Minn.: Capstone
   Books, 1999.

Mead, Sue. *Monster Trucks & Tractors.*
   Race Car Legends. Philadelphia: Chelsea
   House, 1999.

Useful Addresses

Canadian Automobile Sports Club
703 Petrolia Road
Downsview, ON M3J 2N6
Canada

National Hot Rod Association
2035 Financial Way
Glendora, CA 91741

Sports Car Club of America
9033 East Easter Place
Englewood, CO 80112

Internet Sites

Bigfoot
http://www.bigfoot4x4.com

Canadian Motorsports.com
http://www.cmsports.com

Earthquake II
http://www.earthquake2.com

**The Hawaiian Fire Department—
    Jet-Powered Fire Truck**
http://www.jetfiretruck.com

National Hot Rod Association
http://www.nhra.com

Truckworld Online
http://truckworld.com

Index